The Pocket Bible On Protection

Scriptures to Renew Your Mind
and Change Your Life

Harrison House
Tulsa, Oklahoma

Unless otherwise indicated, all Scripture quotations are taken from the *King James Version* of the Bible.

07 06 05 04 03   10 9 8 7 6 5 4 3 2

The Pocket Bible on Protection—
Scriptures to Renew Your Mind and Change Your Life
ISBN 1-57794-593-X (Formerly ISBN 0-89274-834-6)
Copyright © 1995, 2003 by Harrison House, Inc.
P.O. Box 35035
Tulsa, Oklahoma 74153

Introduction

One of the greatest keys to being covered with the protection of God—a covering that cannot be penetrated by the devil—is in the ability to hear the still, small voice of the Spirit of God.

To be in tune with the Spirit of God and alert to His voice, you must know the covenant promises of God—the promises of His Word. God's Word and the still, small voice of the Holy Spirit will always be in agreement.

As you appropriate God's promises of protection by believing, speaking, receiving, and acting upon them, and as you follow the examples of protection in God's Word by angels, Jesus' shed blood, the name of Jesus, the Holy Spirit, and the word of a true prophet (or prophetess), *nothing* will be able to stop you from walking out your God-ordained destiny! Absolutely nothing!

As you meditate in *The Pocket Bible on Protection,* may you be quickened to defy all natural restraints and forcibly head toward the "prize of the high calling of God in Christ Jesus" (Philippians 3:14).

Prayer

Lord Jesus, I thank You for Your divine protection over my life. I thank You for Your angels that watch over me and protect me to keep me safe from harm and injury of any kind. You, Lord, are my refuge and my fortress. I am safe, secure and protected under the shelter of Your wings. I stand upon the promises of Your Word and declare that no evil shall befall me, that no plague shall come near me. Even though I walk through the valley of the shadow of death I will fear no evil because You are with me. Though a thousand may fall at my side and ten thousand at my right hand, they cannot, will not, and shall not come near me. I plead the Blood of Jesus over my life. I thank You, Lord, that Satan is a defeated foe and that he is under my feet. In the Name of Jesus and by the authority of God's Word I come against any assignment arrayed against me by the powers of darkness. I break its power to harm me.

I boldly proclaim that I am protected from the devil's calamities, tragedies, devastation, destruction, anything that he should try to do. Wherever I go and whatever I do, I walk in complete and total security and safety. In Jesus' name, amen.

Protection Scriptures

Old Testament

After these things the word of the Lord came unto Abram in a vision, saying, Fear not, Abram: I am thy shield, and thy exceeding great reward.

Genesis 15:1

And, behold, I am with thee [Jacob], and will keep thee in all places whither thou goest, and will bring thee again into this land; for I will not leave thee, until I have done that which I have spoken to thee of.

Genesis 28:15

And the Lord said unto Jacob, Return unto the land of thy fathers, and to thy kindred; and I will be with thee.

Genesis 31:3

And God sent me before you to preserve for you a remnant in the earth, and to keep you alive by a great deliverance.

Genesis 45:7 NASB

And Moses said to the people, "Do not be afraid. Stand still, and see the salvation of the Lord, which He will accomplish for you today. For the Egyptians whom you see today, you shall see again no more forever.

"The Lord will fight for you, and you shall hold your peace."

Exodus 14:13,14 NKJV

Who is like unto thee, O Lord, among the gods? Who is like thee, glorious in holiness, fearful in praises, doing wonders?

Thou stretchedst out thy right hand, the earth swallowed them.

Thou in thy mercy hast led forth the people which thou hast redeemed: thou hast guided them in thy strength unto thy holy habitation.

Exodus 15:11-13

Behold, I send an Angel before thee, to keep thee in the way, and to bring thee into the place which I have prepared.

Exodus 23:20

I will send a panic in front of you, routing all the nations you reach, until your enemies all turn their backs in flight before you.

Exodus 23:27
Moffatt's Translation

If the Lord delight in us, then he will bring us into this land, and give it us; a land which floweth with milk and honey.

Only rebel not ye against the Lord, neither fear ye the people of the land; for they are bread for us: their defence is departed from them, and the Lord is with us: fear them not.

Numbers 14:8,9

Do not be shocked, nor fear them.

The Lord your God who goes before you will Himself fight on your behalf, just as He did for you in Egypt before your eyes,

And in the wilderness where you saw how the Lord your God carried you, just as a man carries his son, in all the way which you have walked, until you came to this place.

Deuteronomy 1:29-31 NASB

Ye shall not fear them; for the Lord your God he shall fight for you.

Deuteronomy 3:22

And the Lord commanded us to do all these statutes, to [reverently] fear the Lord our God for our good always, that He might preserve us alive, as it is this day.

Deuteronomy 6:24 AMP

When you go to war against your enemies and see horses and chariots and an army greater than yours, do not be afraid of them, because the Lord your God, who brought you up out of Egypt, will be with you.

When you are about to go into battle, the priest shall come forward and address the army.

He shall say: "Hear, O Israel, today you are going into battle against your enemies. Do not be fainthearted or afraid; do not be terrified or give way to panic before them.

For the Lord your God is the one who goes with you to fight for you against your enemies to give you victory."

Deuteronomy 20:1-4 NIV

And it shall come to pass, if thou shalt hearken diligently unto the voice of the Lord thy God, to observe and to do all his commandments which I command thee this day, that the Lord thy God will set thee on high above all nations of the earth:

And all these blessings shall come on thee, and overtake thee, if thou shalt hearken unto the voice of the Lord thy God. . . .

The Lord shall cause thine enemies that rise up against thee to be smitten before thy face: they shall come out against thee one way, and flee before thee seven ways. . . .

The Lord shall establish thee an holy people unto himself, as he hath sworn unto thee, if thou shalt keep the commandments of the Lord thy God, and walk in his ways.

Deuteronomy 28:1,2,7,9

Be strong and of a good courage, fear not, nor be afraid of them: for the Lord thy God, he it is that doth go with thee; he will not fail thee, nor forsake thee.

Deuteronomy 31:6

About Benjamin he said: "Let the beloved of the Lord rest secure in him, for he shields him *all day* long, and the one the Lord loves rests between his shoulders."

Deuteronomy 33:12 NIV

The eternal God is thy refuge, and underneath are the everlasting arms: and he shall thrust out the enemy from before thee; and shall say, Destroy them.

Deuteronomy 33:27

"Be strong and courageous, because you will lead these people to inherit the land I swore to their forefathers to give them. Be strong and very courageous. Be careful to obey all the law my servant Moses gave you; do not turn from it to the right or to the left, that you may be successful wherever you go. Do not let this Book of the Law depart from your mouth; meditate on it day and night, so that you may be careful to do everything written in it. Then you will be prosperous and successful."

Joshua 1:6-8 NIV

For the Lord our God, he it is that brought us up and our fathers out of the land of Egypt, from the house of bondage, and which did those great signs in our sight, and preserved us in all the way wherein we went, and among all the people through whom we passed:

And the Lord drave out from before us all the people, even the Amorites which dwelt in the land: therefore will we also serve the Lord; for he is our God.

Joshua 24:17,18

Stay with me, do not be afraid, for he who seeks my life seeks your life; for you are safe with me.

1 Samuel 22:23 NASB

And he said, The Lord is my rock, and my fortress, and my deliverer;

The God of my rock; in him will I trust: he is my shield, and the horn of my salvation, my high tower, and my refuge, my saviour, thou savest me from violence.

I will call on the Lord, who is worthy to be praised: so shall I be saved from mine enemies.

2 Samuel 22:2-4

In my distress I called upon the Lord, and cried to my God: and he did hear my voice out of his temple, and my cry did enter into his ears.

2 Samuel 22:7

For thou art my lamp, O Lord: and the Lord will lighten my darkness.

For by thee I have run through a troop: *by my* God have I leaped over a wall.

As for God, his way is perfect; the word of the Lord is tried: he is a buckler to all them that trust in him.

For who is God, save the Lord? and who is a rock, save our God?

God is my strength and power and he maketh my way perfect.

He maketh my feet like hinds' feet: and setteth me upon my high places.

He teacheth my hands to war, so that a bow of steel is broken by mine arms.

Thou hast also given me the shield of thy salvation: and thy gentleness hath made me great.

Thou hast enlarged my steps under me; so that my feet did not slip.

2 Samuel 22:29-37

For you have given me strength for the battle and have caused me to subdue all those who rose against me.

You have made my enemies turn and run away; I have destroyed them all.

2 Samuel 22:40,41 TLB

Blessed be God who destroys those who oppose me and rescues me from my enemies. Yes, you hold me safe above their heads. You deliver me from violence.

2 Samuel 22:48,49 TLB

Fear not: for they that be with us are more than they that be with them.

2 Kings 6:16

Jabez cried out to the God of Israel, "Oh, that you would bless me and enlarge my territory! Let your hand be with me, and keep me from harm so that I will be free from pain." And God granted his request.

1 Chronicles 4:10 NIV

Be strong and courageous, be not afraid nor dismayed for the king of Assyria, nor for all the multitude that is with him: for there be more with us than with him:

With him is an arm of flesh; but with us is the Lord our God to help us, and to fight our battles.

2 Chronicles 32:7,8a

On the twelfth day of the first month we set out from the Ahava Canal to go to Jerusalem. The hand of our God was on us, and he protected us from enemies and bandits along the way.

Ezra 8:31 NIV

So the wall was completed on the twenty-fifth of Elul, in fifty-two days. When all our enemies heard about this, all the surrounding nations were afraid and lost their self-confidence, because they realized that this work had been done with the help of our God.

Nehemiah 6:15,16 NIV

You can have hope and feel secure, you can look round you and lie down in safety, lie down with no one to alarm you.

Job 11:18,19a
Moffatt's Translation

But thou, O Lord, art a shield for me; my glory, and the lifter up of mine head.

I cried unto the Lord with my voice, and he heard me out of his holy hill. Selah.

I laid me down and slept; I awaked; for the Lord sustained me.

I will not be afraid of ten thousands of people, that have set themselves against me round about.

Arise, O Lord; save me, O my God: for thou hast smitten all mine enemies upon the cheek bone; thou hast broken the teeth of the ungodly.

Psalm 3:3-7

I will both lie down in peace, and sleep; for You alone, O Lord, make me dwell in safety.

Psalm 4:8 NKJV

Lead me, O Lord, in thy righteousness because of mine enemies; make thy way straight before my face.

Psalm 5:8

But let all those that put their trust in thee rejoice: let them ever shout for joy, because thou defendest them: let them also that love thy name be joyful in thee.

For thou, Lord, wilt bless the righteous; with favour wilt thou compass him as with a shield.

Psalm 5:11,12

O Lord my God, in thee do I put my trust: save me from all them that persecute me, and deliver me.

Psalm 7:1

My shield is God Most High, who saves the upright in heart.

Psalm 7:10 NIV

The Lord also will be a refuge for the oppressed, a refuge in times of trouble.

Psalm 9:9

The Lord replies, "I will arise and defend the oppressed, the poor, the needy. I will rescue them as they have longed for me to do."

The Lord's promise is sure. He speaks no careless word; all he says is purest truth, like silver seven times refined.

Psalm 12:5,6 TLB

Preserve me, O God: for in thee do I put my trust.

Psalm 16:1

The Lord is my rock, and my fortress, and my deliverer, my God, my strength, in whom I will trust; my buckler, and the horn of my salvation, and my high tower.

I will call upon the Lord, who is worthy to be praised: so shall I be saved from mine enemies.

Psalm 18:2,3

He delivered me from my strong enemy, and from them which hated me: for they were too strong for me.

They prevented me in the day of my calamity: but the Lord was my stay.

He brought me forth also into a large place; he delivered me, because he delighted in me.

Psalm 18:17-19

For You will light my lamp; the Lord my God will enlighten my darkness.

For by You I can run against a troop, by my God I can leap over a wall.

As for God, His way is perfect; the word of the Lord is proven; He is a shield to all who trust in Him.

For who is God, except the Lord? And who is a rock, except our God?

It is God who arms me with strength, and makes my way perfect.

He makes my feet like the feet of deer, and sets me on my high places.

He teaches my hands to make war, so that my arms can bend a bow of bronze.

You have also given me the shield of Your salvation; Your right hand has held me up, and Your gentleness has made me great.

You enlarged my path under me, so my feet did not slip.

Psalm 18:28-36 NIV

It is God who avenges me, and subdues the peoples under me;

He delivers me from my enemies. You also lift me up above those who rise against me; You have delivered me from the violent man.

Psalm 18:47,48 NKJV

Now I know that the Lord saves His anointed; He will answer him from His holy heaven with the saving strength of His right hand.

Some trust in chariots, and some in horses; but we will remember the name of the Lord our God.

Psalm 20:6,7 NKJV

For the king trusteth in the Lord, and through the mercy of the most High he shall not be moved.

Psalm 21:7

For he hath not despised nor abhorred the affliction of the afflicted; neither hath he hid his face from him; but when he cried unto him, he heard.

Psalm 22:24

The Lord is my shepherd, I shall not be in want.

He makes me lie down in green pastures, he leads me beside quiet waters, he restores my soul. He guides me in paths of righteousness for his name's sake.

Even though I walk through the valley of the shadow of death, I will fear no evil, for you are with me; your rod and your staff, they comfort me.

You prepare a table before me in the presence of my enemies. You anoint my head with oil; my cup overflows.

Surely goodness and love will follow me all the days of my life, and I will dwell in the house of the Lord forever.

Psalm 23:1-6 NIV

O my God, I trust in thee: let me not be ashamed, let not mine enemies triumph over me.

Shew me thy ways, O Lord; teach me thy paths.

Lead me in thy truth, and teach me: for thou art the God of my salvation; on thee do I wait all the day.

Psalm 25:2,4,5

All the paths of the Lord are mercy and truth unto such as keep his covenant and his testimonies.

Psalm 25:10

Assign me Godliness and Integrity as my body-guards, for I expect you to protect me and to ransom Israel from all her troubles.

Psalm 25:21,22 TLB

But I trust in you, O Lord; I say, "You are my God."

Let me not be put to shame, O Lord, for I have cried out to you; but let the wicked be put to shame. . . .

Psalm 31:14,17 NIV

How great is your goodness, which you have stored up for those who fear you, which you bestow in the sight of men on those who take refuge in you.

In the shelter of your presence you hide them from the intrigues of men; in your dwelling you keep them safe from accusing tongues.

Psalm 31:19,20 NIV

Love the Lord, all his saints! The Lord preserves the faithful, but the proud he pays back in full.

Psalm 31:23 NIV

Thou art my hiding place; thou shalt preserve me from trouble; thou shalt compass me about with songs of deliverance. Selah.

I will instruct thee and teach thee in the way which thou shalt go: I will guide thee with mine eye.

Psalm 32:7,8

Our inner selves wait [earnestly] for the Lord; He is our Help and our Shield.

For in Him does our heart rejoice, because we have trusted (relied on and been confident) in His holy name.

Psalm 33:20,21 AMP

This poor man cried, and the Lord heard him, and saved him out of all his troubles.

The angel of the Lord encampeth round about them that fear him, and delivereth them.

Psalm 34:47

The eyes of the Lord are upon the righteous, and his ears are open unto their cry.

The face of the Lord is against them that do evil, to cut off the remembrance of them from the earth.

The righteous cry, and the Lord heareth, and delivereth them out of all their troubles.

The Lord is nigh unto them that are of a broken heart; and saveth such as be of a contrite spirit.

Many are the afflictions of the righteous: but the Lord delivereth him out of them all.

He keepeth all his bones: not one of them is broken.

Evil shall slay the wicked: and they that hate the righteous shall be desolate.

The Lord redeemeth the soul of his servants: and none of them that trust in him shall be desolate.

Psalm 34:15-22

Plead my cause, O Lord, with them that strive with me: fight against them that fight against me.

Take hold of shield and buckler, and stand up for mine help.

Draw out also the spear, and stop the way against them that persecute me: say unto my soul, I am thy salvation.

Let them be confounded and put to shame that seek after my soul: let them be turned back and brought to confusion that devise my hurt.

Psalm 35:1-4

Trust in the Lord, and do good; so shalt thou dwell in the land, and verily thou shalt be fed.

Delight thyself also in the Lord; and he shall give thee the desires of thine heart.

Commit thy way unto the Lord; trust also in him; and he shall bring it to pass.

And he shall bring forth thy righteousness as the light, and thy judgment as the noonday.

Rest in the Lord, and wait patiently for him: fret not thyself because of him who prospereth in his way, because of the man who bringeth wicked devices to pass.

Cease from anger, and forsake wrath: fret not thyself in any wise to do evil.

For evildoers shall be cut off: but those that wait upon the Lord, they shall inherit the earth.

For yet a little while, and the wicked shall not be: yea, thou shalt diligently consider his place, and it shall not be.

But the meek shall inherit the earth; and shall delight themselves in the abundance of peace.

Psalm 37:3-11

The steps of a good man are ordered by the Lord, and He delights in his way.

Though he fall, he shall not be utterly cast down; for the Lord upholds him with His hand.

Psalm 37:23,24 NKJV

For the Lord loves justice, and does not forsake His saints; they are preserved forever, but the descendants of the wicked shall be cut off.

Psalm 37:28 NKJV

But the salvation of the righteous is of the Lord: he is their strength in the time of trouble.

And the Lord shall help them, and deliver them: he shall deliver them from the wicked, and save them, because they trust in him.

Psalm 37:39,40

I waited patiently for the Lord; and he inclined unto me, and heard my cry.

He brought me up also out of an horrible pit, out of the miry clay, and set my feet upon a rock, and established my goings.

Psalm 40:1,2

Since I am afflicted and needy, let the Lord be mindful of me; Thou art my help and my deliverer; do not delay, O my God.

Psalm 40:17 NASB

Blessed is he that considereth the poor the Lord will deliver him in time of trouble.

The Lord will preserve him, and keep him alive; and he shall be blessed upon the earth: and thou wilt not deliver him unto the will of his enemies.

Psalm 41:1,2

By this I know that thou favourest me, because mine enemy doth not triumph over me.

And as for me, thou upholdest me in mine integrity, and settest me before thy face for ever.

Psalm 41:11,12

Through thee will we push down our enemies: through thy name will we tread them under that rise up against us.

For I will not trust in my bow, neither shall my sword save me.

But thou hast saved us from our enemies, and hast put them to shame that hated us.

Psalm 44:5-7

God is our refuge and strength, a very present help in trouble.

Therefore will not we fear, though the earth be removed, and though the mountains be carried into the midst of the sea;

Though the waters thereof roar and be troubled, though the mountains shake with the swelling thereof. Selah.

Psalm 46:1-3

The Lord of hosts is with us; the God of Jacob is our refuge. Selah.

Come, behold the works of the Lord, what desolations he hath made in the earth.

He maketh wars to cease unto the end of the earth; he breaketh the bow, and cutteth the spear in sunder; he burneth the chariot in the fire.

Be still, and know that I am God: I will be exalted among the heathen, I will be exalted in the earth.

Psalm 46:7-10

Call upon me in the day of trouble; I will deliver you, and you will honor me.

Psalm 50:15 NIV

Behold, God is my helper and ally, the Lord is my upholder and is with them who uphold my life.

He will pay back evil to my enemies; in Your faithfulness [Lord] put an end to them.

Psalm 54:4,5 AMP

As for me, I will call upon God, and the Lord shall save me.

Evening and morning and at noon I will pray, and cry aloud, and He shall hear my voice.

He has redeemed my soul in peace from the battle that was against me, for there were many against me.

Psalm 55:16-18 NKJV

Cast thy burden upon the Lord, and he shall sustain thee: he shall never suffer the righteous to be moved.

Psalm 55:22

What time I am afraid, I will trust in thee.

In God I will praise his word, in God I have put my trust; I will not fear what flesh can do unto me. . . .

In God have I put my trust: I will not be afraid what man can do unto me.

Psalm 56:3,4,11

My heart is fixed, O God, my heart is fixed. I will sing and give praise.

Psalm 57:7

Deliver me from mine enemies, O my God: defend me from them that rise up against me.

Psalm 59:1

I will wait for You, O You his Strength; for God is my defense.

My God of mercy shall come to meet me; God shall let me see my desire on my enemies.

Psalm 59:9,10 NKJV

But I will sing of Your power; yes, I will sing aloud of Your mercy in the morning; for You have been my defense and refuge in the day of my trouble.

To You, O my Strength, I will sing praises; for God is my defense, my God of mercy.

Psalm 59:16,17 NIV

Truly my soul waiteth upon God: from him cometh my salvation.

He only is my rock and my salvation; he is my defence; I shall not be greatly moved.

Psalm 62:1,2

My soul, wait thou only upon God; for my expectation is from him.

He only is my rock and my salvation: he is my defence; I shall not be moved.

In God is my salvation and my glory: the rock of my strength, and my refuge, is in God.

Trust in him at all times; ye people, pour out your heart before him: God is a refuge for us. Selah.

Psalm 62:5-8

But as for me, my prayer is to You, O Lord, in the acceptable time; O God, in the multitude of Your mercy, hear me in the truth of Your salvation.

Deliver me out of the mire, and let me not sink; let me be delivered from those who hate me, and out of the deep waters.

Let not the floodwater overflow me, nor let the deep swallow me up; and let not the pit shut its mouth on me.

Hear me, O Lord, for Your lovingkindness is good; turn to me according to the multitude of Your tender mercies.

And do not hide Your face from Your servant, for I am in trouble; hear me speedily.

Draw near to my soul, and redeem it; deliver me because of my enemies.

Psalm 69:13-18 NKJV

For he shall deliver the needy when he crieth; the poor also, and him that hath no helper.

He shall spare the poor and needy, and shall save the souls of the needy.

Psalm 72:12,13

He guided them with the cloud by day and with light from the fire all night.

Psalm 78:14 NIV

Behold, O God our shield, and look upon the face of thine anointed.

For a day in thy courts is better than a thousand. I had rather be a doorkeeper in the house of my God, than to dwell in the tents of wickedness.

For the Lord God is a sun and shield: the Lord will give grace and glory: no good thing will he withhold from them that walk uprightly.

O Lord of hosts, blessed is the man that trusteth in thee.

Psalm 84:9-12

For thou hast a great love to me, O Lord, saving me from the very depths of death.

Psalm 86:13
Moffatt's Translation

He who dwells in the shelter of the Most High will rest in the shadow of the Almighty.

I will say of the Lord, "He is my refuge and my fortress, my God, in whom I trust!"

Surely he will save you from the fowler's snare and from the deadly pestilence.

He will cover you with his feathers, and under his wings you will find refuge; his faithfulness will be your shield and rampart.

You will not fear the terror of night, nor the arrow that flies by day,

Nor the pestilence that stalks in the darkness, nor the plague that destroys at midday.

A thousand may fall at your side, ten thousand at your right hand, but it will not come near you.

You will only observe with your eyes and see the punishment of the wicked.

If you make the Most High your dwelling— even the Lord, who is my refuge—

Then no harm will befall you, no disaster will come near your tent.

For he will command his angels concerning you to guard you in all your ways;

They will lift you up in their hands, so that you will not strike your foot against a stone.

You will tread upon the lion and the cobra; you will trample the great lion and the serpent.

"Because he loves me," says the Lord, "I will rescue him; I will protect him, for he acknowledges my name.

He will call upon me, and I will answer him; I will be with him in trouble, I will deliver him and honor him.

With long life will I satisfy him and show him my salvation."

Psalm 91:1-16 NIV

Happy is the man who stays by the Most High in shelter, who lives under the shadow of Almighty God,

Who calls the Eternal "My refuge and my fortress, my God in whom I trust"!

He saves you from the fowler's snare and from the deadly pit;

He protects you with his pinions and hides you underneath his wings.

You need not fear the terrors of the night, nor arrows flying in the day,

You need not fear plague stalking in the dark, nor sudden death at noon;

Hundreds may fall beside you, thousands at your right hand, but the plague will never reach you,

Safe shielded by his faithfulness.

You have only to look on and see how evil men are punished;

But you have sheltered beside the Eternal, and made the Most High God your home,

So no scathe can befall you, no plague can approach your tent.

For he puts you under his angels' charge, to guard you wherever you go,

To lift you in their hands lest you trip over a stone;

You can walk over reptiles and cobras, trampling on lions and on dragons.

"He clings to me, so I deliver him; I set him safe, because he cares for me;

I will answer his cry and be with him in trouble, delivering him and honouring him;

I will satisfy him with long life, and let him see my saving care."

Psalm 91:1-16

Mofatt's Translation

Unless the Lord had given me help, I would soon have dwelt in the silence of death.

When I said, "My foot is slipping," your love, O Lord, supported me.

Psalm 94:17,18 NIV

But the Lord has become my fortress, and my God the rock in whom I take refuge.

Psalm 94:22 NIV

Sing a new song to the Eternal, sing, all the earth, to the Eternal, sing to the Eternal, praise him, day after day tell of his saving aid.

Psalm 96:1,2
Moffatt's Translation

You who love the Lord, hate evil! He preserves the souls of His saints; He delivers them out of the hand of the wicked.

Psalm 97:10 NIV

Deliver us, O Lord our God, and gather us from among the nations, that we may give thanks to Your holy name and glory in praising You.

Psalm 106:47 AMP

Then they cried unto the Lord in their trouble, and he delivered them out of their distresses.

And he led them forth by the right way.

Psalm 107:6,7a

Then they cried out to the Lord in their trouble; He saved them out of their distresses.

He brought them out of darkness and the shadow of death, and broke their bands apart.

Psalm 107:13,14 NASB

Then they cried out to the Lord in their trouble; He saved them out of their distresses.

He sent His word and healed them, and delivered them from their destructions.

Psalm 107:19,20 NASB

Be thou exalted, O God, above the heavens. and thy glory above all the earth;

That thy beloved may be delivered: save with thy right hand, and answer me.

Psalm 108:5,6

Give us help from trouble: for vain is the help of man.

Through God we shall do valiantly: for he it is that shall tread down our enemies.

Psalm 108:12,13

Surely he shall not be moved for ever: the righteous shall be in everlasting remembrance.

He shall not be afraid of evil tidings: his heart is fixed, trusting in the Lord.

His heart is established, he shall not be afraid, until he see his desire upon his enemies.

Psalm 112:6-8

O Israel, trust the Lord! He is your helper. He is your shield.

O priests of Aaron, trust the Lord! He is your helper; he is your shield.

All of you, his people, trust in him.

He is your helper, he is your shield.

Jehovah is constantly thinking about us and he will surely bless us. He will bless the people of Israel and the priests of Aaron, and all, both great and small, who reverence him.

Psalm 115:9-13 TLB

From my distress I called upon the Lord; the Lord answered me and set me in a large place.

The Lord is for me; I will not fear; what can man do to me?

The Lord is for me among those who help me; therefore I shall look with satisfaction on those who hate me.

It is better to take refuge in the Lord than to trust in man.

It is better to take refuge in the Lord than to trust in princes.

All nations surrounded me; in the name of the Lord I will surely cut them off.

They surrounded me, yes, they surrounded me, in the name of the Lord I will surely cut them off.

They surrounded me like bees; they were extinguished as a fire of thorns; in the name of the Lord I will surely cut them off.

You pushed me violently so that I was falling, but the Lord helped me.

The Lord is my strength and song, and He has become my salvation.

The sound of joyful shouting and salvation is in the tents of the righteous; the right hand of the Lord does valiantly.

The right hand of the Lord is exalted; the right hand of the Lord does valiantly.

Psalm 118:5-16 NASB

You are my refuge and my shield; I have put my hope in your word.

Away from me, you evildoers, that I may keep the commands of my God!

Sustain me according to your promise, and I will live; do not let my hopes be dashed.

Uphold me, and I will be delivered; I will always have regard for your decrees.

Psalm 119:114-117 NIV

I will lift up mine eyes unto the hills, from whence cometh my help.

My help cometh from the Lord, which made heaven and earth.

He will not suffer thy foot to be moved: he that keepeth thee will not slumber.

Behold, he that keepeth Israel shall neither slumber nor sleep.

The Lord is thy keeper: the Lord is thy shade upon thy right hand.

The sun shall not smite thee *by day,* nor the moon by night.

The Lord shall preserve thee from all evil: he shall preserve thy soul.

The Lord shall preserve thy going out and thy coming in from this time forth, and even for evermore.

Psalm 121:1-8

I lift mine eyes to the mountains; ah, where is help to come from?

Help comes from the Eternal who made heaven and earth.

Never will he let you slip; he who guards you never sleeps; he who guards Israel will neither sleep nor slumber.

The Eternal guards you, sheltering you upon the right; the sun shall never hurt you in the day, nor the moon by night.

The Eternal will guard you from all harm, he will preserve your life;

He will protect you as you come and go, now and for evermore.

Psalm 121:1-8
Moffatt's Translation

"If it had not been the Lord who was on our side," let Israel now say—

"If it had not been the Lord who was on our side, when men rose up against us.

Then they would have swallowed us alive, when their wrath was kindled against us;

Then the waters would have overwhelmed us, the stream would have gone over our soul;

Then the swollen waters would have gone over our soul."

Blessed be the Lord, who has not given us as prey to their teeth.

Our soul has escaped as a bird from the snare of the fowlers; the snare is broken, and we have escaped.

Our help is in the name of the Lord, who made heaven and earth.

Psalm 124:1-8 NKJV

They that trust in the Lord shall be as mount Zion which cannot be removed, but abideth for ever.

As the mountains are round about Jerusalem, so the Lord is round about his people from henceforth even for ever.

Psalm 125:1,2

Blessed is every one that feareth the Lord; that walketh in his ways.

For thou shalt eat the labour of thine hands: happy shalt thou be, and it shall be well with thee.

Psalm 128:1,2

But the Lord is righteous; he has cut me free from the cords of the wicked.

Psalm 129:4 NIV

I will clothe his enemies with shame, but the crown on his head will be resplendent.

Psalm 132:18 NIV

His foes I shroud with dark disgrace, but his own crown shall sparkle.

Psalm 132:18
Mofatt's Translation

Though I walk in the midst of trouble, thou wilt revive me: thou shalt stretch forth thine hand against the wrath of mine enemies, and thy right hand shall save me.

Psalm 138:7

Deliver me, O Lord, from the evil man: preserve me from the violent man.

Keep me, O Lord, from the hands of the wicked; preserve me from the violent man; who have purposed to overthrow my goings.

O God the Lord, the strength of my salvation, thou hast covered my head in the day of battle.

Psalm 140:1,4,7

Surely the righteous shall give thanks unto thy name: the upright shall dwell in thy presence.

Psalm 140:13

Deliver me, O Lord, from mine enemies: I flee unto thee to hide me.

Teach me to do thy will; for thou art my God: thy spirit is good; lead me into the land of uprightness.

Quicken me, O Lord, for thy name's sake: for thy righteousness' sake bring my soul out of trouble.

And of thy mercy cut off mine enemies, and destroy all them that afflict my soul: for I am thy servant.

Psalm 143:9-12

Blessed be the Lord my strength, which teacheth my hands to war, and my fingers to fight:

My goodness, and my fortress; my high tower, and my deliverer; my shield, and he in whom I trust; who subdueth my people under me.

Psalm 144:1,2

The Lord upholdeth all that fall, and raiseth up all those that be bowed down.

Psalm 145:14

The Lord is near to all who call on him, to all who call on him in truth.

He fulfills the desires of those who fear him; he hears their cry and saves them.

The Lord watches over all who love him, but all the wicked he will destroy.

Psalm 145:18-20 NIV

But whoso hearkeneth unto me shall dwell safely, and shall be quiet from fear of evil.

Proverbs 1:33

But safe he lives who listens to me; from fear of harm he shall be wholly free.

Proverbs 1:33
Moffatt's Translation

He stores up sound wisdom for the upright; He is a shield to those who walk in integrity,

Guarding the paths of justice, and He preserves the way of His godly ones.

Proverbs 2:7,8 NASB

Discretion will guard you, understanding will watch over you,

To deliver you from the way of evil, from the man who speaks perverse things;

From those who leave the paths of uprightness, to walk in the ways of darkness.

Proverbs 2:11-13 NASB

My son, let them not depart from your eyes—keep sound wisdom and discretion;

So they will be life to your soul and grace to your neck.

Then you will walk safely in your way, and your foot will not stumble.

When you lie down, you will not be afraid; yes, you will lie down and your sleep will be sweet.

Do not be afraid of sudden terror, nor of trouble from the wicked when it comes;

For the Lord will be your confidence, and will keep your foot from being caught.

Proverbs 3:21-26 NKJV

Forsake her [wisdom] not, and she shall preserve thee: love her, and she shall keep thee.

Proverbs 4:6

The righteous will never be uprooted, but the wicked will not remain in the land.

Proverbs 10:30 NIV

Good men will never be displaced, but the wicked have no footing in the land.

Proverbs 10:30
Moffatt's Translation

The integrity of the upright shall guide them.

Proverbs 11:3a

The righteous is delivered out of trouble, and the wicked cometh in his stead.

Proverbs 11:8

He that keepeth his mouth keepeth his life: but he that openeth wide his lips shall have destruction.

Proverbs 13:3

The lips of the wise shall preserve them.

Proverbs 14:3b

In the fear of the Lord is strong confidence: and his children shall have a place of refuge.

The fear of the Lord is a fountain of life, to depart from the snares of death.

Proverbs 14:26,27

Reverence for God gives a man deep strength; his children have a place of refuge and security.

Reverence for the Lord is a fountain of life; its waters keep a man from death.

Proverbs 14.26,27 TLB

He who ignores discipline despises himself, but whoever heeds correction gains understanding.

Proverbs 15:32 NIV

Pride goeth before destruction, and an haughty spirit before a fall.

Better it is to be of an humble spirit with the lowly, than to divide the spoil with the proud.

Proverbs 16:18,19

A fool's lips bring him strife, and his mouth invites a beating.

Proverbs 18:6 NIV

The name of the Lord is a strong tower the righteous runneth into it, and is safe.

Proverbs 18:10

Do not say, "I will recompense evil"; wait for the Lord, and He will save you.

Proverbs 20:22 NKJV

Man's goings are of the Lord; how can a man then understand his own way?

Proverbs 20:24

Chargers are harnessed for the battle, but saving victory comes from the Eternal.

Proverbs 21:31
Moffatt's Translation

There is no [human] wisdom or understanding or counsel [that can prevail] against the Lord.

The horse is prepared for the day of battle, but deliverance and victory are of the Lord.

Proverbs 21:30,31 AMP

The fear of man bringeth a snare: but whoso putteth his trust in the Lord shall be safe.

Proverbs 29:25

Every word of God is pure: he is a shield unto them that put their trust in him.

Proverbs 30:5

For thou hast been a strength to the poor, a strength to the needy in his distress, a refuge from the storm, a shadow from the heat, when the blast of the terrible ones is as a storm against the wall.

Isaiah 25:4

And thine ears shall hear a word behind thee, saying, This is the way, walk ye in it, when ye turn to the right hand, and when ye turn to the left

Isaiah 30:21

And when you swerve to right or left, you hear a Voice behind you whispering, "This is the way, walk here."

Isaiah 30:21
Moffatt's Translation

And my people shall dwell in a peaceable habitation, and in sure dwellings, and in quiet resting places.

Isaiah 32:18

O Lord, be gracious unto us; we have waited for thee: be thou their arm every morning, our salvation also in the time of trouble.

Isaiah 33:2

For the Lord is our judge, the Lord is our lawgiver, the Lord is our king; he will save us.

Isaiah 33:22

The Eternal himself rules us, the Eternal is our captain, the Eternal is our king, he, he alone, defends us.

Isaiah 33:22
Moffatt's Translation

Strengthen ye the weak hands, and confirm the feeble knees.

Say to them that are of a fearful heart, Be strong, fear not: behold, your God will come with vengeance, even God with a recompence; he will come and save you.

Isaiah 35:3,4

Fear not, for I am with you. Do not be dismayed. I am your God. I will strengthen you; I will help you; I will uphold you with my victorious right hand.

See, all your angry enemies lie confused and shattered. Anyone opposing you will die.

You will look for them in vain — they will all be gone.

I am holding you by your right hand — I, the Lord your God — and I say to you, Don't be afraid; I am here to help you.

Isaiah 41:10-13 TLB

Fear not [there is nothing to fear], for I am with you; do not look around you in terror and be dismayed, for I am your God. I will strengthen and harden you to difficulties, yes, I will help you; yes, I will hold you up and retain you with My [victorious] right hand of rightness and justice.

Behold, all they who are enraged and inflamed against you shall be put to shame and confounded; they who strive against you shall be as nothing and shall perish.

You shall seek those who contend with you but shall not find them; they who war against you shall be as nothing, as nothing at all.

For I the Lord your God hold your right hand; I am the Lord, Who says to you, Fear not; I will help you.

Isaiah 41:10-13 AMP

And I will bring the blind by a way that they knew not; I will lead them in paths that they have not known: I will make darkness light before them, and crooked things straight. These things will I do unto them, and not forsake them.

Isaiah 42:16

Fear not, for I redeem you, I claim you, you are mine.

I will be with you when you pass through waters, no rivers shall overflow you; when you pass through fire, you shall not be scorched, no flames shall burn you.

Isaiah 43:1b,2
Moffatt's Translation

Do not fear, nor be afraid; have I not told you from that time, and declared it? You are My witnesses. Is there a God besides Me? Indeed there is no other Rock; I know not one.

Isaiah 44:8 NKJV

This is what the Lord says: "In the time of my favor I will answer you, and in the day of salvation I will help you; I will keep you and will make you to be a covenant for the people, to restore the land and to reassign its desolate inheritances,

To say to the captives, 'Come out,' and to those in darkness, 'Be free!'

They will feed beside the roads and find pasture on every barren hill.

They will neither hunger nor thirst, nor will the desert heat or the sun beat upon them. He who has compassion on them will guide them and lead them beside springs of water."

Isaiah 49:8-10 NIV

I, even I, am he who comforts you. Who are you that you fear mortal men, the sons of men, who are but grass?

Isaiah 51:12 NIV

Old Testament

I have put my words in your mouth and covered you with the shadow of my hand — I who set the heavens in place, who laid the foundations of the earth, and who say to Zion, "You are my people."

Isaiah 51:16 NIV

The Lord has bared His holy arm in the sight of all the nations, that all the ends of the earth may see the salvation of our God.

Isaiah 52:10 NASB

"Though the mountains be shaken and the hills be removed, yet my unfailing love for you will not be shaken nor my covenant of peace be removed," says the Lord, who has compassion on you.

Isaiah 54:10 NIV

In righteousness you will be established: tyranny will be far from you; you will have nothing to fear. Terror will be far removed; it will not come near you.

If anyone does attack you, it will not be my doing; whoever attacks you will surrender to you.

Isaiah 54:14,15 NIV

"No weapon forged against you will prevail, and you will refute every tongue that accuses you. This is the heritage of the servants of the Lord, and this is their vindication from me," declares the Lord.

Isaiah 5:17 NIV

No weapon forged against you shall succeed, no tongue raised against you shall win its plea. Such is the lot of the Eternal's servants; thus, the Eternal promises, do I maintain their cause.

Isaiah 54:17
Moffatt's Translation

The Lord will guide you always; he will satisfy your needs in a sun-scorched land and will strengthen your frame. You will be like a well-watered garden, like a spring whose waters never fail.

Isaiah 58:11 NIV

Behold, the Lord's hand is not shortened, that it cannot save; neither his ear heavy, that it cannot hear.

Isaiah 59:1

He put on might as armour, and victory as a helmet, and vengeance as his clothing, and zeal to be his mantle.

In strict requital he repays his foes with fury and his enemies with shame, till in the far west men have awe of the Eternal, and in the east they see his brilliant deeds; for his vengeance pours out like a pent-up stream, driven by a blast of wind, but to Zion he comes for deliverance, to free Jacob from its rebels.

As for me, the Eternal declares, this is my compact with them: "My spirit which rests upon you, and the words I have put into your lips, shall never depart from your lips, nor from the lips of your descendants, nor from the lips of their descendants," the Eternal declares, "from henceforth and for ever."

Isaiah 59:17-21
Moffatt's Translation

He will come as a Redeemer to those in Zion who have turned away from sin.

"As for me, this is my promise to them," says the Lord: "My Holy Spirit shall not leave them, and they shall want the good and hate the wrong — they and their children and their children's children forever."

Isaiah 59:20,21 TLB

And I will make thee unto this people a fenced brasen wall: and they shall fight against thee, but they shall not prevail against thee: for I am with thee to save thee and to deliver thee, saith the Lord.

And I will deliver thee out of the hand of the wicked, and I will redeem thee out of the hand of the terrible.

Jeremiah 15:20,21

Blessed is the man that trusteth in the Lord, and whose hope the Lord is.

For he shall be as a tree planted by the waters, and that spreadeth out her roots by the river, and shall not see when heat cometh, but her leaf shall be green; and shall not be careful in the year of drought, neither shall cease from yielding fruit,

Jeremiah 17:7,8

But the Lord is with me as a mighty terrible one: therefore my persecutors shall stumble, and they shall not prevail: they shall be greatly ashamed; for they shall not prosper their everlasting confusion shall never be forgotten.

Jeremiah 20:11

But the Lord is with me like a mighty warrior, so my persecutors will stumble and not prevail. They will fail and be thoroughly disgraced; their dishonor will never be forgotten.

Jeremiah 20:11 NIV

"But I will gather the remnant of My flock out of all countries where I have driven them, and bring them back to their folds; and they shall be fruitful and increase.

"I will set up shepherds over them who will feed them; and they shall fear no more, nor be dismayed, nor shall they be lacking," says the Lord.

Jeremiah 23:3,4 NKJV

"So do not fear, O Jacob my servant; do not be dismayed, O Israel," declares the Lord. "I will surely save you out of a distant place, your descendants from the land of their exile. Jacob will again have peace and security, and no one will make him afraid."

Jeremiah 30:10 NIV

But I will deliver thee in that day, saith the Lord: and thou shalt not be given into the hand of the men of whom thou art afraid.

For I will surely deliver thee, and thou shalt not fall by the sword, but thy life shall be for a prey unto thee: because thou hast put thy trust in me, saith the Lord.

Jeremiah 39:17,18

And they shall dwell safely therein, and shall build houses, and plant vineyards; yea, they shall dwell with confidence, when I have executed judgments upon all those that despise them round about them; and they shall know that I am the Lord their God.

Ezekiel 28:26

For this is what the Sovereign Lord says: I myself will search for my sheep and look after them.

As a shepherd looks after his scattered flock when he is with them, so will I look after my sheep. I will rescue them from all the places where they were scattered on a day of clouds and darkness.

I will bring them out from the nations and gather them from the countries, and I will bring them into their own land. I will pasture them on the mountains of Israel, in the ravines and in all the settlements in the land.

I will tend them in a good pasture, and the mountain heights of Israel will be their grazing land. There they will lie down in good grazing land, and there they will feed in a rich pasture on the mountains of Israel.

I myself will tend my sheep and have them lie down, declares the Sovereign Lord.

I will search for the lost and bring back the strays. I will bind up the injured and strengthen the weak, but the sleek and the strong I will destroy. I will shepherd the flock with justice.

Ezekiel 34:11-16 NIV

Then King Nebuchadnezzar was astonished; and he rose in haste and spoke, saying to his counselors, "Did we not cast three men bound into the midst of the fire?" They answered and said to the king, "True, O king."

"Look!" he answered, "I see four men loose, walking in the midst of the fire; and they are not hurt, and the form of the fourth is like the Son of God."

"Therefore I make a decree that any people, nation, or language which speaks anything amiss against the God of Shadrach, Meshach, and Abed-Nego shall be cut in pieces, and their houses shall be made an ash heap; because there is no other God who can deliver like this."

Daniel 3:29 NKJV

So the king gave the order, and they brought Daniel and threw him into the lions' den. The king said to Daniel, "May your God, whom you serve continually, rescue you!"

A stone was brought and placed over the mouth of the den, and the king sealed it with his own signet ring and with the rings of his nobles, so that Daniel's situation might not be changed. Then the king returned to his palace and spent the night without eating and without any entertainment being brought to him. And he could not sleep.

At the first light of dawn, the king got up and hurried to the lions' den. When he came near the den, he called to Daniel in an anguished voice, "Daniel, servant of the living God, has your God, whom you serve continually, been able to rescue you from the lions?"

Daniel answered, "O king, live forever! My God sent his angel, and he shut the mouths of the lions. They have not hurt me, because I was found innocent in his sight. Nor have I ever done any wrong before you, O king."

The king was overjoyed and gave orders to lift Daniel out of the den. And when Daniel was lifted from the den, no wound was found on him, because he had trusted in his God.

Daniel 6:16-23 NIV

O man greatly beloved, fear not: peace be unto thee be strong, yea, be strong. And when he had spoken unto me, I was strengthened, and said, Let my lord speak; for thou hast strengthened me.

Daniel 10:19

But I will have mercy upon the house of Judah, and will save them by the Lord their God, and will not save them by bow, nor by sword, nor by battle, by horses, nor by horsemen.

Hosea 1:7

And in that day will I make a covenant for them with the beasts of the field, and with the fowls of heaven, and with the creeping things of the ground: and I will break the bow and the sword and the battle out of the earth, and will make them to lie down safely.

Hosea 2:18

And by a prophet the Lord brought Israel out of Egypt, and by a prophet was he preserved.

Hosea 12:13

And it shall come to pass, that whosoever shall call on the name of the Lord shall be delivered: for in mount Zion and in Jerusalem shall be deliverance, as the Lord hath said, and in the remnant whom the Lord shall call.

Joel 2:32

Therefore I will look unto the Lord; I will wait for the God of my salvation: my God will hear me.

Rejoice not against me, O mine enemy: when I fall, I shall arise; when I sit in darkness, the Lord shall be a light unto me.

Micah 7:7,8

The Lord is good, a strong hold in the day of trouble; and he knoweth them that trust in him.

Nahum 1:7

Whatever they plot against the Lord he will bring to an end; trouble will not come a second time.

Nahum 1:9 NIV

"The Lord your God is with you, he is mighty to save. He will take great delight in you, he will quiet you with his love, he will rejoice over you with singing."

"The sorrows for the appointed feasts I will remove from you; they are a burden and a reproach to you.

"At that time I will deal with all who oppressed you; I will rescue the lame and gather those who have been scattered. I will give them praise and honor in every land where they were put to shame."

"At that time I will gather you; at that time I will bring you home. I will give you honor and praise among all the peoples of the earth when I restore your fortunes before your very eyes," says the Lord.

Zephaniah 3:17-20 NIV

For I, saith the Lord, will be unto her a wall of fire round about, and will be the glory in the midst of her.

Zechariah 2:5

So will I save you, and ye shall be a blessing fear not, but let your hands be strong.

Zechariah 8:13b

Turn you to the strong hold, ye prisoners of hope: even to day do I declare that I will render double unto thee.

Zechariah 9:12

The Lord of hosts will defend them; they shall devour and subdue with slingstones. They shall drink and roar as if with wine; they shall be filled with blood like basins, like the corners of the altar.

The Lord their God will save them in that day, as the flock of His people. For they shall be like the jewels of a crown, lifted like a banner over His land.

Zechariah 9:15,16 NIV

And I will rebuke the devourer for your sakes, and he shall not destroy the fruits of your ground;

neither shall your vine cast her fruit before the time in the field, saith the Lord of hosts.

Malachi 3:11

New Testament

Now the birth of Jesus Christ was on this wise: When as his mother Mary was espoused to Joseph, before they came together, she was found with child of the Holy Ghost.

Then Joseph her husband, being a just man, and not willing to make her a public example, was minded to put her away privately.

But while he thought on these things, behold, *the angel of the Lord appeared unto him in a dream,* saying, Joseph, thou son of David, fear not to take unto thee Mary thy wife: for that which is conceived in her is of the Holy Ghost.

And she shall bring forth a son, and thou shalt call his name JESUS: for he shall save his people from their sins.

Now all this was done, that it might be fulfilled which was spoken of the Lord by the
prophet, saying,

Behold, a virgin shall be with child, and shall
bring forth a son, and they shall call his name
Emmanuel, which being interpreted is, God with us.

Then Joseph being raised from sleep did as the
angel of the Lord had bidden him, and took unto
him his wife:

And knew her not till she had brought forth her
firstborn son: and he called his name JESUS.

Matthew 1:18-25

Then Herod, having called the learned men
secretly, ascertained accurately from them the
length of time since the star's appearance, and
sending them to Bethlehem he said, Having proceeded on your way, conduct an exhaustive and
accurate investigation concerning the child, and
after you discover that for which you are seeking,
bring back the news to me in order that I also,
having come, may render homage to him. And
having heard the king, they proceeded on their way.

And behold, the star which they saw in its rising kept on going before them until, having come, it stood above where the young child was. And having seen the star, they rejoiced with great joy, exceedingly. And having come into the house, they saw the young child with Mary, His mother, and having fallen down, they prostrated themselves in homage before Him. And having opened their treasure-chests, they brought to Him gifts, gold, and frankincense, and myrrh. *And having been warned in a dream not to return to Herod, by another road they went back to their country.*

Now, after they had returned, behold, *an angel of the Lord appears in a dream to Joseph,* saying, Having arisen, take at once under your care the young child and His mother and be fleeing into Egypt, and be there until I tell you. For Herod is about to be seeking the young child to destroy Him. And having arisen, he took the young child and His mother under his care by night and withdrew to Egypt.

And he was there until the death of Herod, in order that there might be fulfilled that which was spoken by the Lord through the prophet, saying, Out of Egypt I called my Son.

Matthew 2:7-15
The Wuest New Testament

But Herod having died, behold, *an angel of the Lord appeared in a dream to Joseph in Egypt,* saying, Having arisen, take the young child and His mother under your care and be proceeding into the land of Israel, for those who seek the life of the young child have died.

And having arisen, he took the young child and His mother under his care and went to the land of Israel. However, having heard that Archelaus was reigning as king in Judaea instead of his father, Herod, he was afraid to go there. *And having been warned in a dream,* he withdrew into the regions of Galilee. And having come, he established his home in a city called Nazareth, in order that there might be fulfilled that which was spoken through the prophets, A Nazarene shall He be called.

Matthew 2:19-23
The Wuest New Testament

Remember, I am sending you out as my Messengers like sheep among wolves. So be as wise as serpents, and as blameless as doves. Be on your guard against your fellow men, for they will betray you to courts of law, and scourge you in their Synagogues; and you will be brought before governors and kings for my sake, that you may witness for me before them and the nations.

Whenever they betray you, do not be anxious as to how you shall speak or what you shall say, for what you shall say will be given you at the moment; for it will not be you who speak, but the Spirit of your Father that speaks within you.

Brother will betray brother to death, and the father his child; and children will turn against their parents, and cause them to be put to death; and you will be hated by every one on account of my Name. Yet the man that endures to the end shall be saved. But, when they persecute you in one town, escape to the next; for, I tell you, you will not have come to the end of the towns of Israel before the Son of Man comes.

What I tell you in the dark, say again in the light; and what is whispered in your ear, proclaim upon the housetops. And do not be afraid of those who kill the body, but are unable to kill the soul; rather be afraid of him who is able to destroy both soul and body in Hell.

Are not two sparrows sold for a penny? Yet not one of them will fall to the ground without your Father's knowledge. While as for you, the very hairs of your head are all numbered. Do not, therefore, be afraid; you are of more value than many sparrows.

Matthew 10:16-23,27-31
The Twentieth Century
New Testament

"Through the tender mercy of our God, whereby the Dawn will break on us from Heaven,

"To give light to those who dwell in darkness and the shadow of death, and guide our feet into the Way of Peace."

Luke 1:78,79
The Twentieth Century
New Testament

Do not be afraid, little flock, for your Father has been pleased to give you the kingdom.

Luke 12:32 NIV

But there shall not an hair of your head perish.

Luke 21:18

And you shall know the truth, and the truth shall make you free.

Therefore if the Son makes you free, you shall be free indeed.

John 8:32,36 NKJV

My sheep listen to my voice; I know them, and they follow me; and I give them Immortal Life, and they shall not be lost; nor shall anyone snatch them out of my hands. What my Father has entrusted to me is more than all else; and no one can snatch anything out of the Father's hands. The Father and I are one.

John 10:27-30
The Twentieth Century
New Testament

These things I have spoken unto you, that in me ye might have peace. In the world ye shall have

tribulation: but be of good cheer; I have overcome
the world.

John 16:33

I pray not that thou shouldest take them out of
the world, but that thou shouldest keep them from
the evil.

John 17:15

I do not ask that You will take them out of the
world, but that You will keep and protect them
from the evil one.

John 17:15 AMP

And when Herod was about to bring him out,
that night Peter was sleeping, bound with two
chains between two soldiers; and the guards before
the door were keeping the prison.

Now behold, an angel of the Lord stood by him,
and a light shone in the prison; and he struck Peter
on the side and raised him up, saying, "Arise
quickly!" And his chains fell off his hands.

Then the angel said to him, "Gird yourself and
tie on your sandals"; and so he did. And he said to
him, "Put on your garment and follow me."

So he went out and followed him, and did not know that what was done by the angel was real, but thought he was seeing a vision.

When they were past the first and the second guard posts, they came to the iron gate that leads to the city, which opened to them of its own accord; and they went out and went down one street, and immediately the angel departed from him.

And when Peter had come to himself, he said, "Now I know for certain that the Lord has sent His angel, and has delivered me from the hand of Herod and from all the expectation of the Jewish people."

Acts 12:6-11 NKJV

Then spake the Lord to Paul in the night *by a* vision, Be not afraid, but speak, and hold not thy peace:

For I am with thee, and no man shall set on thee to hurt thee: for I have much people in this city.

Acts 18:9,10

For there stood by me this night the angel of God, whose I am, and whom I serve,

Saying, Fear not, Paul; thou must be brought before Caesar: and, lo, God hath given thee all them that sail with thee.

Wherefore, sirs, be of good cheer: for I believe God, that it shall be even as it was told me.

Acts 27:23-25

For there took a stand at my side this night a messenger of the God whose I am and to whom I render sacred service, saying, Stop fearing, Paul. It is necessary in the nature of the case for you to stand before Caesar.

And behold, God has graciously safeguarded for you all those who are sailing with you. On which account be having courage, men, for I trust God that it shall be in the manner as it has been told me.

Acts 27:23-25
The Wuest New Testament

Consequently, there is now no condemnation to those who are in Christ Jesus.

For the law of the Spirit of life in Christ Jesus made me free from the law of sin and death.

Romans 8:1,2
The Worrell New Testament

If God be for us, who can be against us?

Romans 8:31b

Yet amid all these things we more than conquer through him who loved us!

Romans 8:37
The Twentieth Century
New Testament

Yet amid all these things we are more than conquerors and gain a surpassing victory through Him Who loved us.

Romans 8:37 AMP

Finally, be strong in the Lord, and in the strength of His might.

Put on the full armor of God, that you may be able to stand firm against the schemes of the devil.

For our struggle is not against flesh and blood, but against the rulers, against the powers, against the world forces of this darkness, against the spiritual forces of wickedness in the heavenly places.

Therefore, take up the full armor of God, that you may be able to resist in the evil day, and having done everything, to stand firm.

Stand firm therefore, having girded your loins with truth, and having put on the breastplate of righteousness,

And having shod your feet with the preparation of the gospel of peace;

In addition to all, taking up the shield of faith with which you will be able to extinguish all the flaming missiles of the evil one.

And take the helmet of salvation, and the sword of the Spirit, which is the word of God.

With all prayer and petition pray at all times in the Spirit, and with this in view, be on the alert with all perseverance and petition for all the saints.

Ephesians 6:10-18 NASB

And in nothing terrified by your adversaries: which is to them an evident token of perdition, but to you of salvation, and that of God.

Philippians 1:28

But what things were gain to me, these I accounted loss for Christ.

Nay, more, I even account all things to be loss for the excellency of the knowledge of Christ Jesus my Lord, for whose sake I suffered the loss of all things, and account them refuse, that I may gain Christ.

Philippians 3:7,8
The Worrell New Testament

Who hath delivered us from the power of darkness, and hath translated us into the kingdom of his dear Son.

Colossians 1:13

Therefore, brethren, stand fast, and hold the traditions which ye have been taught, whether by word, or our epistle.

Now our Lord Jesus Christ himself, and God, even our Father, which hath loved us, and hath given us everlasting consolation and good hope through grace,

Comfort your hearts, and establish you in every good word and work.

2 Thessalonians 2:15-17

But the Lord is faithful, who shall stablish you, and keep you from evil.

2 Thessalonians 3:3

The Lord will draw me to himself away from every pernicious work actively opposed to that which is good, and will keep me safe and sound for His kingdom, the heavenly one, to whom be the glory forever and forever. Amen.

2 Timothy 4:18
The Wuest New Testament

Since then the children share in flesh and blood, He Himself likewise also partook of the same, that through death He might render powerless him who had the power of death, that is, the devil;

And might deliver those who through fear of death were subject to slavery all their lives.

For assuredly He does not give help to angels, but He gives help to the descendants of Abraham.

Therefore, He had to be made like His brethren in all things, that He might become a merciful and faithful high priest in things pertaining to God, to make propitiation for the sins of the people.

For since He Himself was tempted in that which He has suffered, He is able to come to the aid of those who are tempted.

Hebrews 2:14-18 NASB

God himself has said—"I will never forsake you, nor will I ever abandon you." Therefore we may say with confidence

"The Lord is my helper, I will not be afraid. What can man do to me?"

Hebrews 13:5b,6
The Twentieth Century
New Testament

Submit yourselves therefore to God. Resist the devil, and he will flee from you.

James 4:7

For he who desires to be loving life and to see good days, let him stop the natural tendency of his tongue from evil, and the natural tendency of his lips to the end that they speak no craftiness, but let him rather at once and once for all turn away from evil and let him do good. Let him seek peace and pursue it, because the Lord's eyes are directed in a favorable attitude towards the righteous, and His ears are inclined unto their petitions, but the Lord's face is against those who practice evil things.

And who is he that will do you evil if you become zealots of the good? But if even you should perchance suffer for the sake of righteousness, you are spiritually prosperous ones. Moreover, do not be affected with fear of them by the fear which they strive to inspire in you, neither become agitated, but set apart Christ as Lord in your hearts, always being those who are ready to present a verbal defense to everyone who asks you for a logical explanation concerning the hope which is in all of you, but doing this with meekness and a wholesome serious caution, having a conscience unimpaired, in order that in the very thing in which they defame you, they may be put to shame, those who spitefully abuse, insult, and traduce your good behavior which is in Christ; for it is better when doing good, if perchance it be the will of God that you be suffering, rather than when doing evil.

1 Peter 3:10-17
The Wuest New Testament

Casting all your care upon him; for he careth for you.

1 Peter 5:7

Casting the whole of your care [all your anxieties, all your worries, all your concerns, once and for all] on Him, for He cares for you affectionately and cares about you watchfully.

1 Peter 5:7 AMP

But, if our lives are lived in the Light, as God himself is in the Light, we have communion with one another, and the Blood of Jesus, his Son, purifies us from all sin.

1 John 1:7
The Twentieth Century
New Testament

To him who is able to keep you from falling and to present you before his glorious presence without fault and with great joy—

To the only God our Savior be glory, majesty, power and authority, through Jesus Christ our Lord, before all ages, now and forevermore! Amen.

Jude 24,25 NIV

And they overcame him by the blood of the Lamb, and by the word of their testimony; and they loved not their lives unto the death.

Revelation 12:11

References

Scripture quotations marked AMP are taken from *The Amplified Bible, Old Testament,* copyright © 1965, 1987 by The Zondervan Corporation, Grand Rapids, Michigan, or *The Amplified Bible, New Testament,* copyright © 1958, 1987 by The Lockman Foundation, La Habra, California. Used by permission.

Verses marked TLB are taken from *The Living Bible* © 1971. Used by permission of Tyndale House Publishers, Inc. Wheaton, Illinois 60189. All rights reserved.

Scripture quotations marked *Moffatt's Translation* are taken from *The Bible, James Moffatt Translation,* copyright © 1922, 1924, 1925, 1926, 1935 by Harper Collins San Francisco; copyright © 1950, 1952, 1953, 1954 by James A. R. Moffatt; and copyright © 1994 by Kregel Publications, Grand Rapids, Michigan.

Scripture quotations marked NASB are taken from the *New American Standard Bible,* copyright © 1960, 1962, 1963, 1968, 1971, 1972, 1973, 1975, 1977 by The Lockman Foundation, La Habra, California.

Scripture quotations marked NKJV are taken from the *New King James Version.* Copyright © 1979, 1980, 1982, Thomas Nelson, Inc.

Prayer of Salvation

God loves you—no matter who you are, no matter what your past. God loves you so much that He gave His one and only begotten Son for you. The Bible tells us that "...whoever believes in him shall not perish but have eternal life" (John 3:16 NIV). Jesus laid down His life and rose again so that we could spend eternity with Him in heaven and experience His absolute best on earth. If you would like to receive Jesus into your life, say the following prayer out loud and mean it from your heart.

Heavenly Father, I come to You admitting that I am a sinner. Right now, I choose to turn away from sin, and I ask You to cleanse me of all unrighteousness. I believe that Your Son, Jesus, died on the cross to take away my sins. I also believe that He rose again from the dead so that I might be forgiven of my sins and made righteous through faith in Him. I call upon the name of Jesus Christ to be the Savior and Lord of my life. Jesus, I choose to follow You and ask that You fill me with the power of the Holy Spirit. I declare that right now I am a child of God. I am free from sin and full of the righteousness of God. I am saved in Jesus' name. Amen.

If you prayed this prayer to receive Jesus Christ as your Savior for the first time, please contact us on the web at www.harrisonhouse.com to receive a free book.

Or you may write to us at
Harrison House
P.O. Box 35035
Tulsa, Oklahoma 74153

Other Harrison House Pocket Bibles

The Pocket Bible on Faith
The Pocket Bible on Healing
The Pocket Bible on Finances

Available from your
local bookstore.

If this book has been a blessing to you
or if you would like to see more of the
Harrison House product line,
please visit us on our website at
www.harrisonhouse.com

Harrison House
Tulsa, Oklahoma 74153

The Harrison House Vision

Proclaiming the truth and the power
Of the Gospel of Jesus Christ
With excellence;

Challenging Christians to
Live victoriously,
Grow spiritually,
Know God intimately.